GW01099330

Original title:
Learning To Love Myself

Copyright © 2024 Swan Charm Publishing
All rights reserved.

Editor: Jessica Elisabeth Luik
Author: Mirell Mesipuu
ISBN HARDBACK: 978-9916-86-046-5
ISBN PAPERBACK: 978-9916-86-047-2

Rekindling Within

Amid the dusk of dreams long cast,
We find the embers of the past,
A spark ignites in silent night,
Reviving hope, a gentle light.

Through shadows dense, we seek our way,
To where the heart's true colors play,
In whispers soft, the soul does sing,
Of rebirth and the joy it brings.

From sorrow's depth, we rise anew,
Like morning's kiss on fields of dew,
The flame within, though dimmed by tears,
Burns brighter through the fading years.

As stars emerge in twilight's sweep,
Their glow within, a promise deep,
The inner flame, with steady breath,
Defies the night, transcends the death.

In every heart, a fire remains,
Unyielding through life's swirling pains,
And in its warmth, a truth we find,
The strength to heal, to bind, to climb.

The Inner Garden's Bloom

Within the heart, a garden lies,
Where hidden flowers greet the skies,
In whispered breeze and sunlight's grace,
They turn to life, a tender space.

The seeds of hope, once lost in time,
Now rise as blossoms, most sublime,
Each petal pure, with colors bright,
Illuminates the darkest night.

Through seasons harsh, their roots endure,
In fertile soil, both rich and pure,
The vines of dreams, they gently weave,
A tapestry of life, they cleave.

In quiet moments, still and clear,
The inner blooms begin to cheer,
A symphony of flora's voice,
Compelling all to heed, rejoice.

With every dawn, the garden grows,
Its beauty in the heart bestows,
A sanctuary, lush and green,
Where spirit thrives, serene, unseen.

Heart's True Haven

In the quiet of the night,
A haven shines so bright.
Where dreams and hopes align,
A sanctuary divine.

Whispers of the past unwind,
Memories gently entwined.
In this place, I am whole,
A refuge for my soul.

Peaceful moments softly sway,
Guiding me through the day.
In heart's true haven, I reside,
Where love and trust abide.

Songs of Self-Gratitude

In the mirror, I see,
A being brave and free.
Thankful for the scars,
They've made me who I are.

Gratitude in every breath,
For each day I have left.
In the rhythm of my voice,
I celebrate my choice.

With each morning's rise,
Grateful for the skies.
Songs of self within me grow,
In gratitude, I glow.

Whispering Winds of Self-Care

Beneath the whispers of the wind,
A gentle strength I find within.
Self-care in every tender breeze,
A healing touch that sets me free.

Moments to pause and just be,
In self-compassion's tranquil sea.
Listening to my heart's soft plea,
In solace, I feel truly seen.

Nurturing dreams with loving grace,
Embracing each day's gentle pace.
On whispering winds, my soul flies,
In self-care's embrace, I rise.

Symphony of My Heart

In the quiet of my mind,
A symphony I find.
Notes of joy and sorrow blend,
In melodies that mend.

Rhythms pulse with newfound grace,
In every heartbeat's gentle pace.
A harmony so pure and sweet,
In life's music, we meet.

Within this symphony's embrace,
I find my sacred space.
In each chord and every part,
I feel the symphony of my heart.

Embracing My Reflection

In the mirror, I stand and see
Each line, each curve, a part of me.
No need to hide, no need to flee,
Here lies my truth, wild and free.

Eyes that gleam with stories told,
A heart of warmth, not bitter cold.
Within my soul, a treasure's gold,
Embracing me, as I grow bold.

Scars and laughter mark my tapestry,
Weaved with grace and tenacity.
Each thread a glimpse of clarity,
In my reflection, I find serenity.

Blossoming in Solitude

In quiet hush of solitude,
I find my bloom, my interlude.
Petals spread in gratitude,
A dance of life, serene and nude.

Cradled in the arms of peace,
I let my whispers softly cease.
From mirrored skies, I find release,
In solitude, my soul's increase.

Time unfolds with gentle grace,
In stillness, I define my pace.
Blossoming in my own space,
A solitary, tender embrace.

Heart's Gentle Embrace

In the silence of the night,
My heart's embrace, a gentle light.
Comfort found in its delight,
Whispered love, honest, tight.

Wrapped in warmth, I breathe anew,
Moments tender, clear, and true.
Heartstrings weave a bond to view,
In embrace, dreams do ensue.

Every beat a loving guide,
Through the valleys, far and wide.
My heart's embrace, my trusted tide,
Washing fear and doubt aside.

Whispers of Self-Acceptance

Echoes in the quiet air,
Hold the whispers, soft and rare.
Gently teaching to beware,
Of self-doubt's deceptive snare.

In the mirror, shadows part,
Seeing clearly, loving heart.
Self-acceptance, tender start,
To embrace and never part.

Each whisper lifts a heavy weight,
Guiding softly to my fate.
In self-love, my spirit sate,
In acceptance, fears abate.

Rediscovering Hope

In shadows cast, a light will spark,
A beacon bright within the dark,
Where dreams once lost, begin to climb,
The steps of hope, through sands of time.

A whisper soft, a gentle breeze,
That stirs the leaves upon the trees,
And in the heart, a seed will grow,
Renewed with strength, the spirit's glow.

Through trials faced, and battles won,
The dawn of hope, like rising sun,
And every tear, and every pain,
Transforms to joy, where hopes remain.

The past once fraught, now fades away,
As hope ensures a brighter day,
With faith restored, and skies so clear,
Rediscovered hope, brings love near.

The Light Within

A lantern glows within the soul,
A guiding light, to make us whole,
It shines through nights of darkest hue,
Revealing paths, and dreams anew.

With every step, this light does grow,
Against the winds, through rain and snow,
It warms the heart, and calms the mind,
A sacred flame, in us aligned.

Though trials come, and shadows loom,
The light within dispels the gloom,
Each flicker bright, a beacon's call,
To rise above, and never fall.

In moments still, and times of haste,
This light within, we must embrace,
For in its glow, we find the way,
To face each dawn, to seize the day.

Loving the Person in the Mirror

Reflected eyes meet gaze's twin,
A journey starts from deep within,
To see the worth, beyond the scar,
And cherish who we truly are.

In every line, and every crease,
Lies strength and beauty, heart's release,
A story told, of trials past,
Yet here you stand, at peace at last.

Embrace the flaws, they make you whole,
Each imperfection, lights the soul,
For loving self, through joy and pain,
Is where true love's essence remains.

With every day, learn to forgive,
To love yourself, is how to live,
And in that mirror, you will find,
A heart that's kind, a soul aligned.

Serenity's Embrace

In quiet woods, where whispers play,
There's peace that waits at break of day,
With rustling leaves and gentle streams,
Serenity wraps us in dreams.

Beneath the sky, so vast and blue,
A calming grace, comes into view,
It soothes the mind, and stills the heart,
From life's turmoil, we depart.

In moments hushed, by nature's side,
All worries cease, the fears subside,
Each breath we take, a soft caress,
Within this calm, we find our rest.

Embracing stillness, calm and pure,
We find the strength, and peace assure,
For in the quiet, love and grace,
We find ourselves, in sweet embrace.

Unfolding My True Essence

Like petals touched by morning dew
I bloom, revealing hidden hue
In sunlight's grace, my spirit flies
Through open skies, where freedom lies

Shedding layers of old disguise
Embracing truth, the spirit cries
In quiet whispers, I find strength
My essence blooms, in full expanse

Within the depths, my heart's refrain
Love's gentle voice, a soft campaign
In every step, my essence grows
Unfolding as the river flows

Dancing with Shadows

Beneath the moon's ethereal light
I dance with shadows in the night
Their whispers merge with silent song
In shadows' arms, I do belong

Through twilight's veil, we move as one
Until the rise of golden sun
In shadows' depths, I find my place
A hidden world, a slow embrace

With every step, a shadowed trace
A dance of darkness, gentle grace
The night reveals what day conceals
In shadows' dance, my soul heals

Path to Self-Kindness

Along a path of tender care
I journey forth, my soul laid bare
With gentle love, I mend the tears
Of weary heart, through time repairs

In every step, a lesson learned
Through self-embrace, my spirit burned
With kindness, strength and softer tone
I walk this path, not on my own

Compassion leads, and I will find
A healing balm for heart and mind
On path to self, I tender grow
In kindness found, a brighter glow

The Art of Being Me

In every brushstroke, color blends
A portrait true, where journey ends
With shades of light and darkened hue
The art of me, both old and new

Through canvas stretched on frame of time
I paint my life, each line a rhyme
With every stroke, my soul reveals
A masterpiece of heartfelt feels

In gallery of life's expanse
In every glance, a second chance
The art of being me, unchained
Unique and free, my spirit gained

Inner Blossoms

Beneath the skin, deep roots entwine,
Where hidden seeds of hope combine.
A garden blooms within the soul,
As petals of the spirit unroll.

In shadows cast by doubts and fears,
Flowers spring from silent tears.
The heart in quiet rooms does bloom,
Transforming every dormant gloom.

With sunlight of compassion's grace,
Each tender leaf finds its place.
Unseen by eyes, true beauty grows,
In whispers soft where kindness flows.

Portrait of Self-Worth

Canvas bold, with colors bright,
I paint my worth in morning light.
With every stroke, a story told,
Of courage bright and heart so bold.

In hues of gold, I find my voice,
In swirls of blue, I make my choice.
To see my value, deep and clear,
Reflects my soul in mirrors near.

The portrait framed by love and grace,
A masterpiece within its space.
Embracing flaws, each contour shows,
The strength from which my spirit grows.

Journey to Self-Discovery

Along the path where shadows play,
I search for truths in light of day.
Each step, a whisper from the past,
To find the core and hold it fast.

Through forests dense and rivers wild,
I seek the wisdom of the child.
In echoes of a laughing breeze,
I find myself with utmost ease.

Mountains high and valleys deep,
Unveil the dreams I long to keep.
The journey's end is yet to see,
But every stride, I learn to be.

The Heart's Own Garden

In the heart's own secret plot,
Where love and tenderness are sought.
A garden blooms with fragrant grace,
In every corner, every space.

Soft petals of forgiveness grow,
In gentle wind, compassion's flow.
The weeds of anger are removed,
As peace within is gently proved.

With every season, lessons learned,
In sun and rain, each leaf has turned.
The heart's own garden, ever green,
Reflects the love that's felt and seen.

Discovering Inner Grace

In silent moments, light unfolds,
A whispering breeze through soul's embrace.
How softly wisdom's tale retold,
We wander in discovering grace.

Amidst the shadows, truth reveals,
A sacred dance of light and dark.
In each enigma, solace feels
The symphony of life's own arc.

Reflections glimmer, pure and bright,
Within the mirrors of our mind.
To glimpse the stars' eternal light,
Is where our truest selves we find.

The river's flow, so clear and pure,
Carries whispers from the past.
Through winding paths, we shall endure,
In every step, inner grace casts.

A dance with time, a timeless song,
In every heartbeat, life renews.
Embrace the moments, fleeting, long,
And find the grace in changing hues.

Flourishing in My Own Essence

Beneath the skies of endless blue,
I breathe the air of sweet release.
In every moment, hope anew,
And find within a sense of peace.

Roots deep in earth, I stand my ground,
As seasons pass, I learn to grow.
In every leaf and petal found,
The essence of my being flows.

A garden blooms within my heart,
With every notion, every dream.
From every tear and joy, I start,
To flourish in my life's own stream.

Under the stars, my spirit beams,
Each constellation whispers clear.
In moonlit nights, in sunlit dreams,
I find my essence, hold it dear.

With open arms, I greet the dawn,
And let my true self show its face.
In every dusk and every morn,
I flourish in my own bright place.

The Heart's Awakening

The dawn's first light, a gentle kiss,
Awakening the heart's deep fire.
In every hue of morning's bliss,
I find the pulse of pure desire.

A melody within the soul,
Resonates through night and day.
In every silence, motions roll,
As heartbeats softly guide the way.

Through valleys deep and mountains high,
The spirit wanders, finds its place.
In every heartbeat, every sigh,
The essence of a vast embrace.

Each whisper of the wind's caress,
Awakens dreams that once were still.
In moments fleeting, happiness,
The heart awakens, finds its thrill.

A symphony of life's true call,
Unfolds within this sacred space.
As heart awakes and breaks the thrall,
It finds in love, a boundless grace.

Whispers of Self-Compassion

In quiet moments, voices speak,
A tender whisper to the heart.
With every breath, no need to seek,
For self-compassion plays its part.

A gentle touch of inner care,
Softens wounds where sorrow's lain.
In every tear, and every prayer,
Compassion's whisper eases pain.

Through trials faced and battles fought,
The spirit cradles wounds with light.
Each tender whisper gently taught,
To love oneself, embrace the night.

Within the soul, a garden grows,
Of self-acceptance, pure and kind.
In every petal, wisdom shows,
The strength in being, peace of mind.

So let the whispers softly sing,
In stillness find your heart's sweet space.
With self-compassion, gently bring,
A love profound to own your grace.

Canvas of Inner Love

In the heart where colors blend,
Soft hues of love ascend,
Brushstrokes gentle, pure, and light,
Painting dreams in the quiet night.

Each pulse a story weaves,
In tender strokes, love believes,
A canvas of feelings unfurled,
Inward beauty within the world.

Whispers of crimson and gold,
In this artistry, hands bold,
Caressing every shadowed part,
Transforming all with loving art.

A symphony of shades unite,
Emerald hopes in dim twilight,
Love's palette, endless and vast,
Eternal art that will always last.

In silence, depths undiscovered,
With each touch, love uncovered,
A masterpiece wrought from above,
Engraved on the canvas of love.

The Healing Verse

In words, a soothing balm,
Whispers in a tranquil calm,
Lines that mend the spirit's tear,
Healing verse beyond compare.

Each syllable a gentle touch,
Meandering, not demanding much,
In the quiet, truths are found,
Sacred in their soft surround.

Heartbreak fades with every line,
In written peace, the soul reclines,
Stitches made with tender prose,
Wounds begin their slow repose.

In pain's release, the heart restored,
Grace in every written chord,
Verses weave a tapestry,
Of quiet strength and bravery.

Words that lift, and words that bind,
With the echoes intertwined,
Rhythmic pulses, hearts converse,
Healing in the form of a verse.

Echoing Inner Kindness

Beneath the surface, kindness dwells,
In silent echoes, it compels,
Whispers of a gentle creed,
In every quiet, selfless deed.

Soft ripples in the brook of time,
Acts profound, yet so sublime,
Inward light, it gently glows,
Shining where compassion flows.

Kindness speaks in simple words,
Through actions more than what is heard,
Echoes through the spaces wide,
In the heart, where love resides.

A tender touch, an open door,
Soft gestures that mean much more,
In every whisper, acts of grace,
Kindness wears a humble face.

These echoes in the soul remain,
In giving, we may ease the pain,
Inward kindness, strength aligned,
Echoes ever intertwined.

My Own Sanctuary

In the quiet of my mind,
A sanctuary, peace I find,
Walls adorned with thoughts serene,
In my refuge, pure and keen.

A solace where my spirit roams,
Inward whispers, gentle poems,
Every breath a soft caress,
Safe within my own fortress.

Turmoil fades beyond the gate,
Peaceful echoes resonate,
In this space, my heart's own prayer,
A sanctuary beyond compare.

Reflections in soft hues imbue,
Tranquility in skies of blue,
In silence, dreams take quiet flight,
In my haven, love alight.

A sacred space where fears release,
Inward peace, a lasting lease,
In my own sanctuary's grace,
Found within this heart's safe place.

Unveiling My Brilliance

In shadows deep, my light unfolds,
A hidden gem of stories told.
Beneath the veil, resplendence shines,
In every heart, this hope aligns.

Awaken now, my radiant gleam,
No longer dim, but bright, supreme.
A beacon through the darkest night,
Guiding souls with newfound sight.

Rise and soar, my spirit high,
No boundaries in this endless sky.
Unveiled, my brilliance boldly gleams,
A symphony of golden dreams.

Eclipsing doubts that once constrained,
My spirit free, untamed, unchained.
In every step, a spark ignites,
Unveiled, my future, bold and bright.

Let brilliance be the guiding star,
Unveiling all of who we are.
In unity, our lights combine,
A tapestry, in which we shine.

Summoning Self-Trust

Within my heart, an echo calls,
To rise above the fear that stalls.
A quiet strength that whispers near,
To trust myself, and never fear.

Through trials faced and battles won,
My inner voice shall not be done.
In self-belief, my spirit soars,
Unlocking all life's hidden doors.

A journey walked on fragile ground,
Yet self-trust grows with every bound.
In every doubt, a seed was sown,
A strength within, now clearly known.

Resilient, strong, my heart suggests,
That self-trust is the truest test.
To trust in me, my path defined,
Through inner trust, my strength aligned.

Summon courage, quiet and still,
With self-trust, I free my will.
In courage born of inner trust,
All doubts and fears shall turn to dust.

Visions of My True Self

In mirror's gaze, my essence sees,
A deeper truth that sets me free.
Not just a face, but soul unmasked,
A vision of the self I've asked.

Through layers thick, the falsehoods shed,
To find the path that lies ahead.
In every flaw, perfection lies,
Through inner sight, my spirit flies.

A journey inward, mapped by heart,
Each vision new, a fresh restart.
True self revealed as shadows fall,
Unveiling light within us all.

No more the masks that cloud my view,
Only the self that's pure and true.
Embracing all, both bright and dark,
A vision true in every spark.

As visions clear, my heart beat strong,
A melody, my inner song.
In true self found, I rise anew,
A vision pure, my spirit true.

Clarion Call of Inner Peace

A gentle calm within me starts,
A clarion call that soothes my heart.
In stillness found, a pure release,
The sacred balm of inner peace.

No tempest wild, no raging sea,
Can drown the peace inside of me.
In silence deep, my soul takes flight,
To realms of calm, serene delight.

Soft whispers of a tranquil mind,
In every breath, this peace I find.
A sanctuary, calm and bright,
A beacon in the darkest night.

With each heartbeat, the silence speaks,
A steady voice that no storm breaks.
The clarion call of peace within,
A harmony where love begins.

In every moment, peace I'll seek,
Its quiet strength makes none seem weak.
The clarion call, forever near,
Of inner peace, so true, so clear.

Serenity in Solitude

In the quiet of the evening,
Where shadows softly play,
I find a peaceful haven,
As night dissolves the day.

The whispering winds allay,
Every worry, every fear,
In solitude, I stray,
To where the mind is clear.

Stars above are gleaming,
With tales of yore untold,
In their light, I'm dreaming,
Of stories not yet old.

Roaming through the silence,
A solace deep I find,
In moments pure and timeless,
My spirit is enshrined.

In solitude's sweet grace,
I meet my inner soul,
In this serene, still space,
I've found what makes me whole.

A Love Reclaimed

Among the ruins of hearts,
Where whispers of old linger,
A new beginning starts,
With love's healing finger.

Once shattered dreams renew,
In twilight's tender glow,
The promises we knew,
In love's revival grow.

With every kiss and sigh,
Old wounds begin to fade,
Underneath the starlit sky,
Our love no longer weighed.

Hand in hand we walk,
On paths once lost and worn,
In silence, we now talk,
Of loves both new and born.

A dance begins anew,
With steps both tried and true,
In love reclaimed and due,
Our hearts their vows renew.

Embracing My Reflection

In the glass, I gaze and see,
Not flaws, but stories told,
A journey meant for me,
In reflections bold.

Lines of laughter, tears of woe,
Etched upon my face,
Each wrinkle, every glow,
Is life's own tender trace.

In my eyes, a spark resides,
Of dreams both lost and found,
In every twist that bides,
A life profound and sound.

I lean in close to view,
The strength beneath the skin,
With love, I now construe,
The joy that lies within.

Embracing my reflection,
With soulful, tender grace,
I find a new direction,
In love's warm, true embrace.

Journey to Self-Acceptance

I walked a path unknown,
Through woods both dark and deep,
In shadows overgrown,
Where silent secrets seep.

Each step a newfound truth,
Of who I am inside,
In the dawn of youth,
No longer will I hide.

Mountains tall and steep,
I climbed with trembling hand,
Learning as I leap,
Where courage makes a stand.

In valleys low and wide,
Where echoes softly call,
I left my doubts aside,
Embracing every fall.

Now standing in the light,
With heart and spirit free,
On this infinite flight,
I've learned to just be me.

Breathing in Acceptance

Inhale the dawn, exhale the night,
Feel the stillness, embrace light.
With every breath, let worries fade,
Accept the path that life has laid.

Heartbeats whisper tales untold,
Stories of strength and courage bold.
In the mirror, find peace and grace,
Acceptance smiles upon your face.

Through the tempest, through the calm,
Know you're held within love's palm.
In every sigh, in every prayer,
Life breathes a song beyond compare.

Self-Written Symphony

Notes of wonder start to play,
In life's orchestra every day.
Each choice, each step, a melody,
Creating our own symphony.

Strings of hope and drums of will,
Waves of passion never still.
In concert with dreams we glide,
Crafting music far and wide.

With each refrain, more piece revealed,
In every soul a song is sealed.
We write, we sing, in harmony,
Our self-made, pure symphony.

Stepping into My Light

Shadows fade, dawn's embrace,
Courage found in this place.
Every step, a new delight,
As I move into my light.

Clouds drift by, stars emerge,
Empowered now by inner surge.
Walking paths both wild and rare,
In light I find the strength to dare.

With each stride, the darkness flees,
Brightness whispers through the trees.
Stepping firm, embracing sight,
Fully now, I own my light.

The Petals of Me

In the garden of my soul,
Petals unfurl, stories unfold.
Colors rich and scents so sweet,
Mirroring life in each heartbeat.

Thorn and blossom, dual embrace,
Growth through struggle, beauty's face.
Roots run deep, anchored strong,
Petals whisper life's own song.

In the weave of greens and dew,
Every petal tells what's true.
In the bloom, the world can see,
The endless petals that are me.

Dancing with My Soul

In the quiet of the night,
My spirit starts to soar,
Whispers of forgotten dreams,
Echo from the core.

A waltz with shadows cast,
Yet light in every turn,
Steps of hope and memories,
In tandem, we discern.

Boundaries fade and blend,
To rhythms only known,
A choreography of existence,
In this dance, I'm not alone.

Through trials and tribulations,
With grace, I navigate,
In every twirl and spin,
My soul and I relate.

The dance with my spirit,
Eternal, pure, and free,
In the music of my essence,
My soul dances with me.

Canvas of Inner Strength

Upon the canvas of my heart,
Colors start to flow,
Bold strokes of resilience,
In hues only I know.

Each line and curve a testament,
To battles hard and won,
The masterpiece is forming,
With each rise of the sun.

Brushes dipped in patience,
Shades of hope appear,
The art of life's endurance,
Unfolds serene and clear.

Faint whispers guide the strokes,
In tones both soft and bright,
A tapestry of courage,
Emerges from the night.

The canvas of my inner strength,
A portrait of my strife,
In every stroke and color,
I paint the story of my life.

Gardening My Heart

In the garden of my soul,
Seeds of dreams I sow,
With tender care and patience,
Love begins to grow.

Each emotion like a flower,
Blossoms in due time,
Through sunshine and through showers,
Life's rhythms shape the rhyme.

Weeds of doubt may whisper,
Amongst the vibrant green,
But with vigilant devotion,
My heart remains serene.

Seasons come in cycles,
Some harsh, and others kind,
Yet even in the winter,
Strength within I find.

In gardening my heart,
Growth and grace align,
With every bloom and petal,
I tend this heart of mine.

Crowning My Own Essence

In the mirror's silent vow,
I see my power gleam,
A crown of self-assurance,
Worn not just in a dream.

With every step of wisdom,
Each lesson learned with grace,
I claim my royal presence,
In every time and place.

Beneath this crown I fashion,
Strength and beauty grow,
An emblem of my journey,
Through valleys high and low.

No need for outside sanction,
For worth is self-declared,
The essence of my being,
In every pulse is bared.

Crowning my own essence,
With dignity and pride,
In the kingdom of my spirit,
My truth I cannot hide.

Renewal of Inner Joy

In silence, blooms the quiet heart,
A garden where new hopes do start.
With gentle winds, the soul does sway,
In morning's light, a brighter day.

Each dawn renews the golden hues,
With laughter in each drop of dew.
From shadows past, the spirits fly,
And find new wings to touch the sky.

Lost melodies now drift in song,
As rivers cleanse what felt so wrong.
A canvas fresh with colors bright,
We paint anew with love's pure light.

With every step, a rhythm found,
In nature's arms, we're safe and sound.
Beneath the stars, dreams intertwine,
In this renewal, joy is mine.

Cultivating Self-Respect

In mirrors, truths reflect so clear,
Our worth within, we hold dear.
With every flaw, a perfect gem,
In self-respect, we bloom again.

The seeds of pride we slowly sow,
In kindness, we shall surely grow.
With gentle hands, we lift the soul,
To find itself complete and whole.

In voices strong, we hear our name,
A testament to break the shame.
The roots run deep, the branches wide,
In self-respect, we do abide.

Nourish the heart with love and care,
In every breath, we find repair.
With open eyes, the world we greet,
In self-respect, we are complete.

Roots of Inner Beauty

In quiet soils, our beauty grows,
Beneath the ground where no one knows.
The roots entwine in silent grace,
A hidden strength within our space.

Through tender shoots, our spirits rise,
Drawn upward to the open skies.
With petals soft, we touch the air,
In silent bloom beyond compare.

No storm can tear these roots apart,
For deep they run within the heart.
In every leaf, a story told,
Of inner beauty, pure and bold.

Embrace the self in shadowed light,
Within the dark, we find our might.
For inner beauty never fades,
With roots that hold through life's parades.

Waves of Self-Discovery

Upon the shores of dreams untold,
We walk the sands, both young and old.
With every wave, a whisper true,
Of who we are and what we knew.

The tides of time reveal the path,
In every laugh and teardrop's bath.
Through crashing storms and seas serene,
We find the self, the in-between.

The horizon calls with colors bright,
A journey's end within our sight.
Each lesson learned, a treasure found,
In waves of self, where we are bound.

Through every ebb, the heart expands,
As life unfolds in shifting sands.
In depths unknown, the soul will dive,
In self-discovery, we thrive.

Echoes of Authenticity

In mirror's gaze, a true face seen,
Reflections pure, unmarked by scene,
Voices quiet, a soul's own plea,
Echoes carry authenticity.

Behind the mask, the heart exposed,
No pretense worn, no truth opposed,
In silence deep, the whispers free,
Echoes dance with authenticity.

In every step, a claim to own,
The roads traversed, the seeds we've sown,
Among the stars, our spirits flee,
Reflecting echoes, authenticity.

A gentle breeze, a secret told,
A tender tale of actions bold,
In dreams and wakeful eyes to see,
Every shadow sings authenticity.

In life's vast quilt, each stitch a part,
A tapestry spun from the heart,
Interwoven, loose yet fastened, be,
Threads that bind with authenticity.

Soft Light of Presence

Beneath the dawn, the world awakes,
In tender breaths, the morning breaks,
A whisper soft, a calm presents,
In every glow, the essence blends.

The sun ascends with gentle sweep,
Its fingers touch, in silent keep,
In light's embrace, all worries cease,
Presence whispers, tender peace.

The trees sway slow, in rhythm's grace,
Leaves flutter soft, in light's embrace,
Each moment birthed, a gift intense,
Cradled in the soft presence.

Amid the noise, the world spins fast,
But here and now, the stillness lasts,
A tranquil heart, in the suspense,
Awakening, the light of presence.

In every breath, a story spun,
Beneath the moon, beneath the sun,
Gently held, our fears dispense,
Bathed in the soft light of presence.

The Warmth of Self-Trust

Amid the storms, the gales we face,
An inner voice, a calming space,
In shadows long, we find the thrust,
A guiding flame, the warmth of trust.

Through valleys deep, o'er mountains high,
The pulse within, a beckoned cry,
When doubts encroach and fears combust,
We're shepherded by self-trust.

In every trial, in each stride,
The answers gleaned from deep inside,
No path too dark, no journey thrust,
That's not warmed by rays of trust.

A faith enkindled in the core,
Not seeking less, but yearning more,
A quiet strength, a voice robust,
Encased within the warmth of trust.

United within, no force divides,
In self-belief, a soul abides,
In every heartbeat, calm and just,
Grows ever pure, the seed of trust.

Becoming Whole

Through shattered dreams, through broken ties,
We weave anew beneath the skies,
From pieces scattered, we console,
In each fragment, becoming whole.

In quietude, in silent nights,
We gather strength, embrace new heights,
Amidst the cracks, there grows a soul,
In healing light, becoming whole.

From shadows dense, to light's return,
Through lessons lived, we dare to learn,
Each wound a tale, each scar a scroll,
In journey's end, we're becoming whole.

With every tear, a bridge we form,
In hearts that mend, in spirits warm,
From broken halves, a seamless goal,
Together we are becoming whole.

In every breath, in every beat,
In trials cold, in victories sweet,
We rise, we fall, in ebb and flow,
Forever thus, becoming whole.

Unlocking Inner Harmony

In the quiet, whispers sing
A calm that cloaks the storm within
With every breath, let peace take wing
Unlock the door where dreams begin

Let chaos fade, let tensions cease
Feel the rhythm of your soul
Through mindful steps, attain release
In unity, become whole

Silent echoes, inner grace
A dance where joy and anguish met
In the sanctuary of this space
Find the harmony still yet

Balance rests in whispered thought
A symphony without tune
In this tranquil spot you've caught
A harmonious afternoon

Let your spirit waltz and sway
To the music of the mind
Let the calm light your way
In inner harmony, you'll find

Bathing in Self-Kindness

Gentle whispers, tender care
Treat yourself like morning dew
Bathe in kindness, softly share
With the person that is you

Every tear a healing rain
Washing wounds of wear and strife
Let compassion ease the pain
Breathing love back into life

Self-forgiveness, gentle touch
Cradle hopes like newborn light
You are worthy of so much
In your sight, love's reignite

Let each flaw become a jewel
In the crown of your own grace
Banish voices, harsh and cruel
In your kindness, find your place

Soak in waters pure and kind
From your essence, gently spring
In self-kindness, peace you'll find
As your heart begins to sing

Embrace yourself with open arms
In the bath of self-delight
Find the warmth that softly charms
'Neath the moonlight, pure and bright

Breaking the Chains of Doubt

In shadows deep where doubts reside
A flicker of hope yet gleams
With courage as your trusted guide
Break the chains, and grasp your dreams

Fear not the darkness of unknown
Unveil the strength that lies within
In the fight, you are not alone
Believe, and let the light begin

Each step forward, strength reclaim
Let the doubt begin to wane
Feel the rush of inner flame
Burning bright, igniting gain

In the mirror, reflection see
A warrior unbowed, so stout
With each breath, set your soul free
Ever breaking chains of doubt

Rise above the stormy calls
Ignore whispers of disdain
Stand where light of courage falls
And break free from every chain

Beneath the Surface

Deep within the ocean's heart
Where light scarce finds its way
Beneath the waves, a hidden art
Colors dance in muted play

In unseen depths, life intertwines
With mysteries that shadows shroud
In velvet depths that softly shine
Silence speaks, though never loud

Beneath the surface, stories weave
Silent tales of ancient days
In currents, whispered dreams believe
While surface waves in sunlight blaze

Here, where time seems slow and still
Secrets drift on currents cold
In silent depths, the heart can fill
With wisdom from the times of old

Dive into the unseen realms
Where silent songs of life abound
Beneath the surface, hope embarks
In echoes never making sound

Tender Reflections

In the quiet of the evening's glow,
Memories flutter like autumn leaves,
Whispers of the past softly flow,
In the heart that quietly grieves.

Gentle echoes of laughter remain,
Lingering like a sweet, fading song,
Shadows of joy, mingled with pain,
In tender reflections, where we belong.

Time holds hands with love's embrace,
Carving moments in the soul's deep well,
In the mirror of a beloved face,
Stories only our hearts can tell.

Beneath the stars, dreams intertwine,
With the gentle touch of the night,
In tender reflections, we find the sign,
Of love's enduring, soft-spoken light.

As moonlight bathes the sacred ground,
We cherish memories, ever so dear,
In endless waves, our hearts are bound,
By reflections tender, near and clear.

Uncharted Self-Love

In a sea of dreams, I cast my net,
Seeking shores of love unknown,
With every sunrise, a new mindset,
And a heart that's grown, all my own.

Winds of doubt may billow strong,
Yet my sails are set with grace,
Navigating through right and wrong,
Finding peace in my own embrace.

Under skies vast and adorned,
With whispers of self-worth's glow,
Every scar and joycorn,
Charting paths where I must go.

No map for this inner quest,
Only stars that guide so true,
With each step, I do my best,
To honor the me I once knew.

In the mirror of the ocean's gaze,
Reflections of love unfold,
In uncharted self-love's endless maze,
I find a compass made of gold.

Inner Sanctuary

Amid the noise of life's parade,
A quiet haven, deeply sought,
Beneath the shade that dreams have made,
A sanctuary in my thoughts.

Whispers of peace in gentle streams,
Flow through valleys of the mind,
In the quiet corners of my dreams,
Pure tranquility, I find.

Walls adorned with memories dear,
Of moments tender, blissful, sweet,
In this haven, far from fear,
Soul and heart in silence meet.

Candles flicker in the sacred space,
With light that dances, soft and warm,
Inner sanctuary's tender grace,
Shelters from life's storm.

In this realm, where I am true,
Peace is born from inner light,
Renewed with every passing view,
Soul's refuge in the quiet night.

Flourishing from Within

From seeds of doubt, potential springs,
In the soil of hope, deeply sown,
With every challenge, strength it brings,
In life's garden, deeply grown.

Sunlight of love, with tender rays,
Nurtures roots, so firm and strong,
Blossoming in countless ways,
To a melody, life's own song.

Rain of wisdom, pure and fine,
Feeds the soul's enduring grace,
In every drop, a sacred sign,
Of flourishing in every space.

Leaves unfold in vibrant hues,
Whispers of courage softly spoken,
In the dance of morning dews,
Chains of the past, gently broken.

In the garden of the heart,
Petals of joy begin to spin,
Every end, a bold new start,
A journey flourishing from within.

Heartfelt Solitude

In silence, I find solace
Two hearts, one spirit, in quiet prose
A dance of thoughts in twilight's fold
Where secrets speak and tales unfold

A whisper to the evening air
Beneath the moon's enchanted glare
The soul's embrace in night's embrace
In heartfelt solitude, my grace

The stars align with inner peace
In solitude, my fears release
No shadows cast, no burdens bear
Only tranquil breaths of tender care

A moment's pause in time's cascade
Where dreams and memories serenade
here solitude's soft lullaby
Gently lifts me to the sky

No lonely path, no empty hall
In solitude, I hear the call
Of whispered truths and silent beams
In heartfelt solitude, love gleams

Unconditional Belonging

In the embrace of hearts so true
Where skies are wide, and skies are blue
No bounds constrain the love that's shared
In this world, we are prepared

Belonging in the souls we touch
In gentle hands, that mean so much
No storm can break this bond so tight
Unconditional, pure and bright

Through seasons change and tempests roar
We find a place, forevermore
In eyes that see our boundless worth
In every corner of this earth

Beyond all faults and broken ways
We shine together in countless days
Where every flaw is understood
In unconditional, boundless good

Together, with a love so strong
We find a place where we belong
No questions asked, no need to prove
In this embrace, we find our groove

Gentle Waves of Acceptance

In the quiet, in the calm
Where worries fade, and fears disarm
Soft whispers of the ocean's call
Where acceptance gently drapes us all

Waves that kiss the sandy shore
Embrace our hearts forevermore
No need to change, no need to hide
In gentle waves, we find our stride

The sea reflects a tranquil peace
Where doubts and fears may gently cease
In its embrace, we find our place
With love's sweet touch, we feel grace

Every ripple, every tide
Carries tales of lives inside
With open arms, the sea extends
In gentle waves, acceptance blends

We stand together, side by side
In harmony, with the ocean's glide
With each wave's gentle caress
We find our place, in love's endless

Finding My Own Rhythm

In the quiet of the dawn
A melody begins to spawn
A heartbeat's pace, a soul's reprise
In rhythm, life's magic lies

The journey twists, the road unwinds
In every step, our truth defines
Through highs and lows, the tempo flows
In each moment, courage grows

Listening to the inner beat
Where heart and soul in harmony meet
The world fades, and truth remains
In my own rhythm, joy sustains

Through chaos, silence finds its place
With every breath, I find my grace
A dance of life, a sacred tune
In rhythm's light, I find the moon

No need to chase another's song
In my own rhythm, I belong
With every step, a path anew
Finding rhythm, finding true

The Gift of Self-Acceptance

In the mirror's quiet gaze,
I see a truth, a tender trace,
Wrinkles, scars that softly maze,
Each line, a journey I'd embrace.

Perfection's mask, I set aside,
To greet the flaws I would abide,
For in my heart, where truths collide,
I find the strength, I do not hide.

The whispers of the world, they fade,
No longer by their words, I'm swayed,
In quiet, peaceful self-parade,
I walk the path that I have made.

Embrace the shadows and the light,
In every flaw, a new insight,
My history, my soul's delight,
In every weakness, I find might.

With each acceptance, love renews,
My heart, my soul, in brighter hues,
A gift that blooms in varied views,
In self-acceptance, peace ensues.

Unveiling My True Self

Behind the masks I've learned to wear,
A blossoming, a life laid bare,
In silent whispers, truths declare,
Unveiling self beyond compare.

Layers shed in courage gained,
Heart and spirit unrestrained,
Through struggles faced and battles waged,
True self, in freedom, now displayed.

With every truth that I reveal,
A bond of strength I start to feel,
In honesty, I slowly heal,
My veiled self I now repeal.

No longer bound by past disguise,
In open view, I seek the skies,
With authentic heart, I rise,
Unveiling self in every eye.

Through every tear and laughing smile,
I journey on, one step, one mile,
Unveiled, I am my own exile,
In true self, I reconcile.

Nurturing My Spirit

Within the quiet of my mind,
A garden blooms, a space confined,
In still tranquility, I find,
A peace that nurtures, undefined.

With gentle hands, I tend the soil,
In patience, learning to uncoil,
My spirit, free from worldly toil,
In inner calm, I find my foil.

Each moment spent in silent grace,
I strengthen roots in sacred place,
To grow, to bloom, in time and space,
A spirit nurtured, finds its pace.

In whispers of the night and day,
I listen to what heartstrings say,
In nurturing, I learn to sway,
My spirit dances, free to play.

With every breath, in peace, I dwell,
In nurturing, my strengths excel,
A loving space I start to tell,
My spirit's song, a grateful spell.

Harmony with Myself

In quiet moments, soft and still,
I seek the tunes my heart fulfills,
A gentle symphony, at will,
In harmony, my spirit thrills.

With every breath, in sync, in line,
I find a rhythm, pure, divine,
In melodies of heart and mind,
A peace within, I seek and find.

The shadows dance with light so bright,
In harmony, they play, unite,
In balance, day and calmest night,
My inner self takes gentle flight.

Through pain and joy, through high and low,
I learn to sway, to let it flow,
In harmony's embrace, I grow,
At peace with self, I gently glow.

Within this dance of life and soul,
In harmony, I find my whole,
In every note, I find control,
At peace within, my spirit's goal.

Healing from Within

In the silence, wounds begin to fade,
Where whispers of the heart are laid.
Through tears, resilience is born,
In night's embrace, we are reborn.

Shadows cast by yesterday's plight,
Dissolve in morning's tender light.
Each scar a story, each ache a song,
In struggle's grip, we grow strong.

The soul's tapestry, woven tight,
Through pain, we gain newfound sight.
With every whisper, every breath,
Steps toward life, away from death.

Inward journeys, where truth resides,
Where fear retreats and hope abides.
The heart's echoes, no longer thin,
We find our healing from within.

Sculpting My Soul

From raw stone, a vision gleams,
Carved by dreams and silent streams.
Chisels of time, in gentle sway,
Shape the form, night and day.

Each strike, a lesson, each flake, a clue,
Crafting the self, pure and true.
Softened edges, roughened core,
Sculpting deeper, seeking more.

In the marble's depth, secrets hide,
Patience unwraps what's inside.
Contours of soul, smooth and bright,
Emerging from the shadows of night.

Hands of life, precise and bold,
With each touch, the story is told.
With every flaw, with every whole,
Eternity molds sculpting my soul.

Growing Into My Own

With each dawn, a petal unfurls,
Vibrant hues in life's twirls.
Roots dig deep in earth's embrace,
Reaching up, finding place.

Through seasons' shift, I bend and sway,
Learning grace in night and day.
Storms may break, but strength is sown,
In the soil, growing into my own.

Leaves may fall, with wisdom's gain,
From their loss, beauty remains.
Each wrinkle, a tale, each line, a trace,
In time's mirror, I find my face.

Blossoms bloom in wrinkles' weave,
Ephemeral, as we believe.
With each moment, essence shown,
In nature's dance, growing into my own.

The Mirror's Revelation

Gaze deep into the glassy pane,
Reflections whisper, naught in vain.
Eyes that seek, truths unveiled,
Inner echoes, often trailed.

Each glance, a story intertwined,
Of battles fought, and peace aligned.
With every crack, a sign revealed,
The soul exposed, once concealed.

Shadows dance in silent prose,
Mingling light where darkness goes.
In the mirror's depth, secrets wane,
Revelations, without shame.

Reflections bear the weight of time,
A silent witness, pure and prime.
In its surface, lives are penned,
In the mirror's revelation, we transcend.

Sanctuary in My Own Skin

In the shelter of my being
I find solace, peace foreseeing
A haven where I truly begin
A sanctuary in my own skin

A whisper of self-kindness flows
Creating space where love shows
Within these bounds, courage grows
As I plant every seed that sows

The layers peel to bare my truth
In this refuge, I reclaim my youth
Embrace the scars and search for proof
That here, I am enough, forsooth

No storm can breach my sacred walls
Not trials, nor the world's harsh calls
My heart's fortress, it never stalls
In my own skin, I stand tall

Each breath births a new rebirth
In my sanctuary, I find worth
An inner realm where dreams unearth
The treasure of my soul's girth

Tender Path to Self-Affection

Softly treading paths within
Where self-love does begin
A road that's tenderly spliced thin
With threads of joy and akin

In gentle whispers, self-love speaks
Through valleys, hills, and peaks
It mends the spaces, cracks, and leaks
Where once, fragility reeked

Unfolding flowers in my chest
Nourished by the love I invest
This path, by kindness, is blessed
A love that doesn't need a test

To hold myself in warm embrace
Granting grace, giving space
Each step, a loving, tender trace
On this path, I find my place

Weaving strength through every breath
A tender path that fosters depth
In self-affection, I find wealth
A journey marked by inner health

Resilience of My Heart

Through the storm and driving rain
My heart endures, concealing pain
Its pulse, a rhythm to sustain
The courage born from every strain

In the darkness, it finds light
A beacon burning day and night
With every challenge, every fight
My heart emerges stronger, bright

Resilience flows through veins of steel
A testament to wounds that heal
Each scar narrates the strength I feel
The fortress built from sheer will

No tear can drown, nor loss can break
A heart that knows what's at stake
Each beat, a promise I remake
Resilient hearts can never quake

In quiet moments, I'll reflect
On trials faced and self-respect
My heart, with resilience, decked
A testament to love, direct

Silent Embrace of Myself

In the stillness of the night
I find my own internal light
A silent embrace, holding tight
Forgiving shadows out of sight

The world retreats, and I am here
With whispered musings near
A sanctuary, free from fear
Where self-love can reappear

I cradle every thought and dream
In silent moments, they redeem
A gentle touch, a tender gleam
Of self-compassion's flowing stream

In silence, I learn to listen
To the tears that softly glisten
A silent embrace, my heart christen
With love that does not imprison

Embracing all, the light and dark
Each silent moment leaves a mark
Within myself, I find the spark
Of love's quiet, healing arc

Tender Roots of Self-Affection

In the soil where I am sown,
Tender roots begin to grow.
Beneath the earth, a world unknown,
Is where my self-affection flows.

Each root seeks the morning sun,
Through layers deep, through darkness spun.
Nurtured by the work I've done,
Tender roots, my love's begun.

Patience brings the blooming grace,
Petals open, warm embrace.
In this garden, I will trace,
Tender roots and find my place.

Whispers in the breeze I hear,
Soft and gentle, calm and clear.
From within, my heart draws near,
Tender roots dissolve my fear.

Grounded in this sacred place,
Beauty shows a tender face.
Firmly held, I interlace,
Tender roots, my self-affection's grace.

Rediscovering My Worth

In the mirror, I now see,
A soul who shines so fervently.
Through trials past, and wounds set free,
Rediscovering who I am meant to be.

Each scar a mark of battles won,
Each tear a river towards the sun.
In every pain, my strength begun,
Rediscovering, I am the one.

With every breath, I claim my right,
To stand in love, to hold the light.
A heart once heavy, now takes flight,
Rediscovering, it's pure delight.

In whispered truths, my spirit sings,
Of endless dreams and boundless wings.
With open heart, the joy it brings,
Rediscovering, life brightly rings.

Found in silence, peace unfurls,
A tapestry of unseen pearls.
In newfound worth, my life swirls,
Rediscovering, love within me twirls.

Sanctuary of the Heart

In the quiet, there I find,
A sanctuary, so aligned.
Within my heart, the stars unwind,
A sacred space, profoundly kind.

No walls to build, no doors to close,
In this haven, my spirit flows.
A boundless realm where love bestows,
Sanctuary, where my soul grows.

Gently cradled, dreams take flight,
In the soft embrace of night.
Within this space, I feel the light,
Sanctuary, oh so bright.

Here, no fears or shadows stay,
Only love to guide my way.
In peaceful silence, I do sway,
Sanctuary, come what may.

In the stillness of my core,
I find a truth I can't ignore.
Safe and cherished, I explore,
Sanctuary, forevermore.

Bouquet of Self-Respect

A garden blooms within my soul,
A place where countless petals dole.
With every step, I take control,
Bouquet of self-respect, my goal.

Each flower here, a lesson learned,
Each thorn, a boundary I've discerned.
In every bloom, my heart has yearned,
Bouquet of self-respect, I've earned.

Through seasons harsh, through storms and rain,
I've tended to this growing lane.
In every loss, I've found my gain,
Bouquet of self-respect, my plain.

Petals soft yet standing strong,
In quiet grace, they all belong.
Each fragrance sings a mindful song,
Bouquet of self-respect, lifelong.

In this arrangement, I now see,
The beauty of my dignity.
With head held high, my spirit free,
Bouquet of self-respect, I decree.

The Mirror's Truth

In the glass, I see a tale,
Of dreams both frail and bright.
A world where whispers sail,
Through mornings and the night.

Reflections often change,
Yet hold a constant hand,
Showing me the range,
Of who I truly am.

In depths, I find a smile,
Echoes of my core,
Even if for a while,
I forget what I adore.

Through tears and bitter fear,
A courage finds its way,
The mirror stands so clear,
Guiding me each day.

With heart aligned in truth,
I'll face what life will bring,
In the mirror, I find my youth,
And the strength to spread my wings.

Becoming My Own Hero

In the quiet of my mind,
A whisper grows to shout,
To leave the past behind,
And face the world no doubt.

Paths of courage, once so dim,
Now beckon me to see,
That strength lives deep within,
In every part of me.

Armor forged from every tear,
And battles fought alone,
The hero I hold dear,
Is in my heart and bone.

With faith in every stride,
I'll journey through the night,
Embracing all my sides,
And walking towards the light.

Becoming what I seek,
In every step I choose,
I'll find the will to speak,
And never fear to lose.

Healing My Heart

The dawn breaks with a tear,
Yet softly brings the sun,
A new day to revere,
Where healing has begun.

The scars that mark my soul,
Remind me of my fight,
In pieces, I am whole,
Growing through the night.

In acceptance, there's a cure,
For every wound and pain,
In love so warm and pure,
I'll find myself again.

With each breath that I take,
I mend the fractures deep,
Awakening to make,
A promise I will keep.

To heal my heart each day,
With kindness as my guide,
In every gentle way,
I feel my spirit rise.

Discovering Inner Beauty

Beneath the surface, there's a light,
A gem that's seldom seen,
In shadows, burning bright,
A beauty pure and keen.

No mirror can reflect,
The depth of what's inside,
A grace that takes effect,
When fears no longer hide.

In silence, it's revealed,
A strength so subtle, near,
With patience, wounds are healed,
And beauty becomes clear.

Through trials and the rough,
True colors start to show,
In moments kind and tough,
Inner beauty starts to glow.

Embracing every flaw,
With love that's truly rare,
I stand in quiet awe,
Of the beauty I now wear.

Nurturing My Spirit

In the dawn of new beginnings,
A gentle calm does arise.
Whispers of ancient wisdom,
Echo through vast skies.

Roots delve deep in soil,
Embracing all they've known.
Branches stretch toward heavens,
With love they've always grown.

Silent prayers in moments still,
Nourish the heart anew.
The soul's lantern, faint but bright,
Guides the path so true.

Each breath a gentle promise,
Of strength to see it through.
In the dance of life's rich tapestry,
Faith and love imbue.

Nurturing the spirit inside,
With patience, grace, and care.
In the heart of every challenge,
A new dawn meets us there.

Revelation of My True Colors

In the mirror's silver whisper,
Reflections start to bloom.
Every hue, a story,
Escaping from my room.

Once concealed in shadows,
Now boldly they emerge.
Each color paints a portrait,
Of soul's unsteady surge.

Reds of passion, blues of peace,
Yellows bright as day.
Greens of growth, and purples deep,
In their embrace, I sway.

Through the mosaic of my being,
True colors intertwine.
Courage breaks the barriers,
Creating space to shine.

In the revelation of my essence,
No fear, no hiding place.
Here I stand, in full spectrum,
With dignity and grace.

Embers of Inner Joy

Beneath the silent evening sky,
A flicker starts to glow.
Embers of a hidden joy,
In the heart's gentle flow.

Warmth that rises quietly,
From deep within the soul.
Guiding lights in darkened nights,
Towards an unseen goal.

Whispers of a silent laugh,
Echos in the mind.
Moments lived in pure delight,
In memories, we find.

In the dance of shadows cast,
A smile begins to grow.
Embers softly, brightly burn,
In an ever constant show.

Through trials and through victories,
Their spark will never die.
Embers of inner joy persist,
Beneath the vastest sky.

Eclipsing Shadows of Insecurity

In the twilight of self-doubt,
Shadows start to loom.
Eclipsing rays of confidence,
Creating pockets of gloom.

But within the heart's deep chamber,
A steady light remains.
Guiding through the darkest fear,
Transcending all the pains.

In whispers soft but certain,
Strength begins to rise.
Dispelling clouds that covered,
With faith's unwavering ties.

Each shadow faced with courage,
Begins to fade away.
Eclipsing only momentarily,
Before the break of day.

Beyond the veil of insecurities,
Lies a spirit bold and free.
Eclipsing shadows conquered,
Revealing the true me.

Strength in Vulnerability

In moments when my heart feels weak,
I find the courage there to speak.
The whispered fears I now set free,
Reveal the strength inside of me.

Through teardrops shed and shadows deep,
A hidden fortitude I keep.
With every crack I dare unveil,
In openness, I never fail.

This aching heart, with tender scars,
Illuminates like distant stars.
Each spoken truth, each bared soul part,
Proclaims the power of a heart.

No armor shields, no walls surround,
In vulnerability, I'm found.
For strength is not in steel or stone,
But in the courage felt alone.

In peaceful silence, I embrace,
The gentle power in this space.
With fearless steps, I now declare,
That strength in love is laid bare.

Embracing My Flaws

Imperfections, they define,
A tapestry of threads, so fine.
Each thread a story, woven clear,
A mark that's cherished, held dear.

In every flaw, a tale unfolds,
Of courage, battles, love retold.
They are the stars that light my night,
In darkest hours, they shine bright.

No mask I wear, no false pretense,
For flaws reveal my true essence.
With each mistake, I learn and grow,
A dance of life, a constant flow.

The mirrors show a face in truth,
Of wisdom gained through trials of youth.
I stand complete, not lacking grace,
In every scar, I find my place.

So here's to flaws in all their might,
Embraced with joy, with pure delight.
For in these cracks, the light pours through,
Creating me, creating you.

The Blooming Heart

Within my chest, a garden blooms,
A myriad of vibrant hues.
With each heartbeat, a petal grows,
In rosy dawn and twilight glows.

The flowers sway in tender breeze,
A symbol of my spirits ease.
With roots that delve the deepest earth,
They find the source of love's birth.

Through sunlit days and storm-torn skies,
My heart endures, it never dies.
With every pain, with every tear,
New blossoms rise, dispelling fear.

This verdant space within my core,
Holds dreams and wishes, evermore.
The seasons change, yet constant stays,
The blooming heart in myriad ways.

A garden tended with pure care,
Flourishes in open air.
For in this space of love and grace,
I find my joyful, blooming place.

Seeds of Self-Compassion

Within the soil of tender mind,
I plant the seeds of care, so kind.
With gentle words and soft embrace,
I nurture growth within this space.

These seeds of love begin to sprout,
Dispelling shadows of self-doubt.
With each new leaf a tender strain,
A melody of self-sustained.

Through storms and droughts, they persevere,
The roots of self-love growing near.
In every trial, a lesson found,
In self-compassion, I am bound.

This garden blooms with patient grace,
In every petal, find my place.
With every tear and tender touch,
I heal this heart I love so much.

For in the seeds of love I sow,
A radiant garden starts to grow.
In self-compassion, I've discovered,
A flourishing heart, uncovered.

Embrace of Solitude

In the silence of the night,
Where stars whisper light,
I find a peaceful, fleeting gaze,
In solitude's gentle embrace.

The world's noises fade away,
In stillness, I gently sway,
Each breath a soft caress,
In solitude, I find my rest.

Whispers of trees become my friends,
In this solitude, healing mends,
A dance with shadows on the wall,
In solitude, I stand tall.

No rush of time, no hurried pace,
Just me in this cherished space,
A moment pure, undefined,
In solitude, I unwind.

Echoes of a distant song,
In solitude, I belong,
Each beat a gentle guide,
In solitude, I confide.

Cherishing My Inner Light

In the dark, a flicker bright,
Guiding me through endless night,
A tender glow to softly see,
The light within belongs to me.

Shadows dance but can't conceal,
The sparks of life I deeply feel,
A glow that whispers stories old,
This inner light, a tale untold.

Amongst the chaos, pure and true,
A light that evermore will do,
To hold me high, to lead me through,
My inner light, my soul's debut.

No storm can douse, no winds can sway,
This light that turns the night to day,
Cherishing with each heartbeat,
My inner light, so pure and sweet.

In moments lost, it finds my way,
This guiding warmth, a gentle ray,
Ever present, softly bright,
Cherishing my inner light.

Warming to Myself

In the quiet of dawn's first gleam,
I breathe with hope, I softly dream,
A warmth within begins to rise,
With each sunrise, my heart's surprise.

Mirror's gaze reflects a face,
Bathed in tender, gentle grace,
A smile blooms, pure and kind,
Warming to myself, my mind.

Through life's ebbs and constant flows,
A newfound warmth forever grows,
In moments tender, bold, and clear,
Warming to myself, sincere.

Shadowed pasts no longer fright,
In self-embrace, I find the light,
Each scar a story, each tear a part,
Warming to my honest heart.

With gentle whispers, self bestowed,
In kindness, my soul is sowed,
In every step, with every breath,
Warming to myself, my depth.

Finding Home Within

In quiet nooks where shadows play,
I find a place, a heart's array,
A home built not of stone and wood,
But where my spirit understood.

Walls of love and ceilings wide,
A refuge found in deep inside,
Each corner whispers sweet refrain,
In solitude, there is no pain.

Finding home within the calm,
Where soul's embrace is soothing balm,
A place to rest, to heal, to grow,
In inner realms, my heart's aglow.

Amidst the noise and outward chase,
Within I find my sacred space,
A map of love, a path so clear,
Finding home, so close, so near.

With every breath, I see it true,
A home within is born anew,
No need to wander, seek, or roam,
For in myself, I've found my home.

The Phoenix Within Me

In the ashes of my past I lie
Reborn anew with a fiery cry
Wings aflame, I rise with might
A beacon blazing in the night

From embers dark, my spirit wakes
A phoenix heart that never breaks
With every fall, I learn to soar
Stronger, brighter than before

Through trials fierce, I find my way
In rebirth's embrace, I choose to stay
Flames consume but also give
A chance to die, a chance to live

In gaps between what was and will
I gather strength, I bend my will
For each demise, a start unfolds
A tale of might that life upholds

No longer bound by shadows cold
A radiant force, a story told
From cinders softly, I proclaim
The phoenix in me burns untamed

Self-Whispered Secrets

In quiet moments, I convene
With whispers soft, my inner dream
Secrets shared with heart alone
A world within I've always known

Gently spoken truths reveal
Layers hidden, wounds to heal
In solitude, I find my voice
A silent pact, my sacred choice

Through hushed confessions, shadows fade
I navigate the paths I've made
Whispers curl in twilight's air
A binding spell with tender care

Beneath the surface, currents speak
Of strength restored, of courage meek
In whispered terms, I understand
The silent grasp of heart and hand

Self-whispered secrets guide my way
In twilight's hush, they softly lay
With every breath, I come to see
The depth of silence, setting me free

Mending the Fractures

In life's mosaic, pieces torn
Fractures carved where dreams were born
Through shards of hurt, I seek to find
The gentle art of hearts aligned

Fragments hold the tears we've cried
Yet in the breaks, pure light resides
With every piece, a story told
Of strength and love that we uphold

Hands that mend with tender grace
A broken past we can embrace
Healing comes with time's embrace
A gentle hand, a softer place

Bits of sorrow, threads of gold
In scars, a beauty yet untold
Through every break, we find a way
To knit the light of every day

In mending fractures, we reveal
The woven quilt of wounds that heal
In unity, our hearts renew
In every fracture, love shines through

Echoes of Self-Love

In whispers soft of love's embrace
I find the stillness, sacred space
Echoes tender, gently sing
The boundless love within they bring

Each spoken word, a mirror's touch
Reflecting worth within so much
In echoes pure, my heart replies
To self with love, through truth-filled eyes

In silent echoes, love resounds
In inner peace, where calm surrounds
Self-love whispers, sweet and clear
A guiding light, forever near

Through echo's call, I come to see
The endless well of love in me
A trace of grace, a whisper deep
In love's embrace, my soul to keep

Every echo, soft and true
A promise made, a vow renewed
To love myself in every way
In echoes pure, I'll always stay

Empowering My Own Voice

In the silence, I find my song,
A melody that's true and strong.
No longer bound by doubt and fear,
My voice rings out, loud and clear.

Through trials, I have come to know,
The power within can truly grow.
With every word, my spirit frees,
Unfurling like the wind-swept trees.

I cast aside the shadows' claim,
Emerging brighter, shedding blame.
For in my depths, the truth is mine,
No longer to be undermined.

With courage, I embrace my sound,
A symphony that knows no bound.
Each note a testament to me,
My voice, my strength, my liberty.

So here I stand, in light and grace,
Empowered in life's grand embrace.
Unyielding, sure of where I stand,
My voice, a beacon through the land.

Harmony with My Spirit

I seek the quiet of the mind,
A place where thoughts in peace unwind.
Where echoes of my heart's own song,
Flow gently like a brook along.

In nature's whispers I find calm,
A sweet and ever-soothing balm.
Each breath I take, a gift, a prayer,
Aligning with the love held there.

I dance in rhythms of the earth,
Connected to my soul's own worth.
In harmony with life's own beat,
I find my place, I feel complete.

The stars, they shine within my core,
Guiding me to ever more.
No longer lost in worldly fuss,
I am enough, I am just right for us.

My spirit sings in notes divine,
In harmony, our hearts align.
A sacred song, a life's embrace,
With every breath, I find my space.

The Resurrection of Self-Belief

In darkest nights, I've walked alone,
Each step, a tremor through the bone.
Doubt whispered often, clear and loud,
Yet I emerged from shadowed clouds.

From ashes of despair, I rise,
A phoenix rare beneath new skies.
In heart and mind, belief reborn,
A light within, no longer torn.

No chains to bind, no fears to quake,
With each new dawn, my soul awake.
I am the captain of my fate,
The master of my own estate.

With every trial, strength I gain,
In every loss, there is a flame.
It fuels the fire of my belief,
Transforming pain into relief.

So here I stand, unshaken, free,
A testament to what can be.
The seed of hope within me sown,
Resurrected, my worth now known.

Serenade to My Being

Inward I turn, to find my song,
A serenade where I belong.
In valleys deep, on peaks so high,
My spirit sings, I touch the sky.

My essence flows with every note,
In harmony, I am afloat.
No need for masks, nor need for shame,
I am enough, just as I claim.

Through whispered words and silent sighs,
I hear my truth, no need for lies.
With every beat, my heart reveals,
A love so pure it gently heals.

Every flaw, a mark of grace,
Each scar a story I embrace.
For in this dance of life, I see,
A symphony that is all me.

In gratitude, I lift my voice,
Embracing all, the pain, the joys.
This serenade, a gift, a plea,
To cherish all that I can be.

Treasuring My Own Company

In the quiet of my space,
I find solace in my mind.
No need for the world's embrace,
In my own peace, I am aligned.

Laughter echoes in my heart,
Even when I'm all alone.
Every moment, a fresh start,
In solitude, I've truly grown.

Books and dreams I'll explore,
Voyaging through inner seas.
Rediscovering what's in store,
In the company of me.

Mirrors show a face so bright,
Shedding fears from days long gone.
In my presence, I find light,
In my truth, I now belong.

Every whisper, every thought,
Becomes music gently played.
In my own love, I am caught,
In my own world, unafraid.

The Dawn of Self-Worth

Morning sun graces my skin,
Touched by warmth, I rise anew.
In my heart, strength lies within,
Confidence in every hue.

Gone are days of seeking praise,
Validation I now create.
In my presence, sunlight stays,
Casting shadows, small and great.

Every step with purpose strides,
Fear and doubt fade into mist.
On this journey, I confide,
In myself, I now exist.

No longer bound by past grief,
In my bloom, I find release.
Claiming love, my own belief,
In this dawn, I find my peace.

With each day, my worth unfolds,
Like a flower kissed by dawn.
In this truth, my heart upholds,
Self-worth in me reborn.

Inner Blossoming

From the seed of silence deep,
Sprouts of dreams and hopes arise.
In my heart, these roots I keep,
Reaching ever toward the skies.

Petals open to the sun,
In my soul, a garden grows.
Inner blossoming begun,
Where my spirit freely flows.

Nourished by the love inside,
Each new day brings gentle care.
In this growth, no need to hide,
Blooming bright, my heart laid bare.

Seasons come and seasons pass,
Still, my essence stands in bloom.
In the mirror, life's amass,
Filling up each empty room.

In this garden that is me,
Flowers tell a story grand.
Infinite and wild, yet free,
By my own light, I will stand.

The Lantern within Me

In the darkest nights I face,
Glows a lantern deep inside.
Guiding me through time and space,
In its warmth, I choose to bide.

Flickers of my inner truth,
Light the path where shadows lay.
In this glow, I find my youth,
Holding fears and doubts at bay.

Never needs this light to dim,
In my heart, forever bright.
Whispered winds or tempests grim,
The lantern steadies through the night.

In its beam, I see my soul,
Reflections of a life well-spent.
Showing me I am made whole,
In this glow, my spirit's sent.

Carrying hope, a steady flame,
Lighting worlds that can't be seen.
In the lantern lives my name,
A beacon in the deepest dream.

Milton Keynes UK
Ingram Content Group UK Ltd.
UKHW020857280624
444593UK00019B/65